MIDWIFE OF THE WILD FRONTIER

Melissa Tyler - Luciana Maruca

Written by Melissa Tyler
Ilustrated by Luciana Maruca

Cover: Luciana Maruca

ISBN:9798862805543

About the Author

Melissa Tyler, Patty's 4th great granddaughter, was driven to understand why her ancestor made the choices she did. She pored over Patty's diaries, family histories, and retraced her steps through Maine in order to make sense of her polyandrous and polygamist grandmother.

About the Illustrator

Luciana started drawing in her childhood and never stoped. At some point she tried to "get serious" and graduated as a graphic designer. Since that didn´t fulfill her artistic needs, she went back to college and became a comic book designer. She´s been coloring, drawing and writing comic books ever since.

PREFACE

I grew up with stories of my pioneer ancestors. Many were related to me, but some were not, yet they were all connected to me by my religion. I was taught to be inspired by their sacrifice and faith. Patty Bartlett Sessions was the magical ancestor that was not only directly related to me, but also a prominent figure of idealized pioneers from my lessons. She was not only a person of great faith, but one that contributed to her society in meaningful and needed ways and also one who contributed to history with her record keeping.

As I grew older and saw the complexities of religion, human behavior, and what we teach as truth; I wanted to learn for myself, straight from the pioneering midwife's pen, what she thought of it all and why she made the choices she did. So, I read Patty's published journals. It took two years studying what at times were really boring passages, only to be delighted when I came across fascinating details. However, I knew that if I wanted my daughters to learn about Patty, I might have more success if I turned the more intriguing parts into a graphic novel.

So, here is her story in all the humor I could create around what were sometimes hard and disturbing details. I now have my own impressions on Patty's motives and desires. I am sure other readers will come up with their own conclusions.

Melissa Tyler

The events in this story really did happen. The order of events has been rearranged in some cases. The dialogue has been invented unless otherwise noted in the footnotes. This book is not to be used for historical reference, even though it contains the truth of Patty's story. Use it to get to know who she really was and how she worked in her world. Cold hard facts can be found in Patty's personal published diaries.

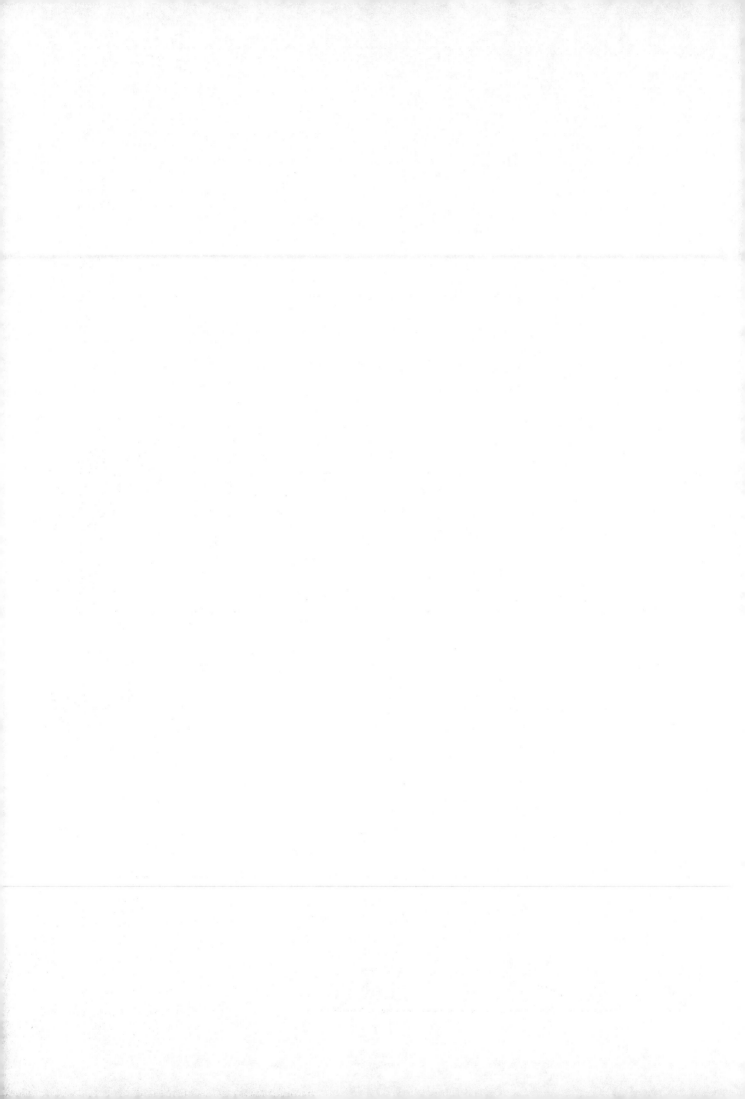

MY PARENTS WERE ENOCH BARTLETT AND MARTHA ANNA HALL.

I KNOW WHAT YOU'RE THINKING, BUT 26 IS NOT THAT YOUNG.

HEY!

I WAS MY MOTHER'S FIRST BABY BUT WAS MY FATHER'S 11TH. AFTER HIS FIRST WIFE DIED, MY FATHER MARRIED MY 26-YEAR-OLD MOTHER ANNA.

HE EVENTUALLY HAD A TOTAL OF 20 KIDS. NOT ALL SURVIVED. *

HE MUST HAVE BEEN A HANDSOME 52.

ME!

WILL IT BE CONFUSING TO HAVE SIBLINGS THE SAME AGE AS YOUR OWN CHILDREN OR YOUNGER?

NO, NO, THAT'S COMMON FOR THIS DAY AND AGE.

IT WILL BE COMMON FOR THE FUTURE TOO, EXCEPT SPOUSES WON'T DIE, THEY'LL JUST GET DIVORCED.

DO WE ALL HAVE TO CALL HER MOM?

MY MOTHER LIVED JUST OVER 100 YEARS.

I MANAGED TO SURVIVE AND OUTLIVE MORE THAN HALF OF THEM, HA! BETCHA DIDN'T THINK I'D LIVE TO SEE THE INVENTION OF THE STEAM TRAIN! TOO BAD I NEVER GOT TO RIDE IN ONE.

*Different records give differing number of total kids. Perhaps it is hard to count them all when after one dies, the next child is given the same name.
Asa was 30 yrs, Reuben 26, Relief 25, Submit 23, Betsey 20, Burry 19, Thankful 18, Olive 15, Lucy 13 years at the time of Anna and their Father Enoch's marriage.

PATTY
I WAS A YOUNG AND WISE 26 YEAR OLD WHEN I MARRIED YOUR FATHER. COULDN'T YOU JUST WAIT A LITTLE BEFORE GETTING MARRIED!

MOM, 26 IS CONSIDERED AN OLD MAID AND YOU MARRIED A 52 YEAR OLD. DAVID IS 22. DON'T MAKE ME MARRY AN OLDER MAN!

MY PARENTS DIDN'T APPROVE OF MY CHOICE (*), SO I DID WHAT ANY LOVE SICK AND IRRATIONAL GIRL WOULD DO.

I RAN AWAY AND MARRIED HIM.

BY "RAN AWAY" I MEAN WE WENT TO LIVE WITH HIS PARENTS.

NICE TO HAVE YOU HERE. WE HAVE SO MUCH WORK WE COULD USE YOUR HELP WITH!

MIND IF I PAY IN BOVINE AND COTTON DAVID? DOLLAR BILLS HAVEN'T BEEN INVENTED YET. **

HI PATTY, I'M HOME. I GOT PAID IN COW TODAY.

OH GOOD! NOW I CAN MAKE BUTTER! BY THE WAY, WHILE YOU WERE GONE I WOVE THE BED SHEETS, STUFFED PILLOWS AND A MATTRESS WITH CATTAILS, AND THEN TIED THE ROPES FOR THE BED.

THEN I FORAGED THROUGH THE WOODS, CLIMBED A TREE AND COLLECTED SOME HONEY AND WAX. MADE SOME CANDLES, SHEARED THE SHEEP AND CARDED THE WOOL. SPUN THE WOOL INTO THREAD AND AM NOW WEAVING THE MATERIAL SO YOU CAN WEAR THE PANTS TOMORROW!

*We don't know the reasons why Anna and Enoch were against Patty's marriage to David. Patty said that her parents threatened to cut her off from any help from them and were true to their word. Patty, according to Patty, helped out her other siblings financially in their marriages. Patty's father said with regret before he died, "Oh Patty, you made a good choice, better than I should have made for you." (Women's Exponent issues: 13 (September 1, 1884) 51:13 (september 15, 1884): 63;13 (November 1, 1884):86;13 (November 15, 1884): 94-95;13 (February 1, 1885): 134-35; 13 (March, 1885): 150-51;14 (June 1, 1885): 2,14 (November 15, 1885):85-86, 94-95)

**The name "dollar" is a transliteration of a german coin from "Joachimsthal" in the Czech republic. People shortened this to Thaler → Dollar. Alexander Hamilton introduced the dollar as the national currency in 1792. At that time, the most commonly used currency was the Spanish peso. Green backs- or dollar bills came into circulation during the Civil War. The idea of which was first introduced by Patty's future son in law.

*Patty never begrudged her in laws and taking care of them. It seemed the natural thing to do and she didn't complain.

PEOPLE MOVED IN AND OUT OF TOWNS AS OPPORTUNITIES AROSE OR WHEN TIMES WERE HARD.

PATTY, I CAN'T TAKE THIS LOOM WITH ME. WOULD YOU BUY IT OFF ME?

HOW MUCH?

HOW DOES $4 SOUND?*

PERFECT, SOLD!

YES! THIS MEANS I'LL BE THE ONLY WEAVER FOR MILES!

THANK GOODNESS THERE ARE MORE WAYS TO BRING HOME THE BACON THAN ACTUALLY KILLING THE PIG!

I WAS THE ONLY ONE CAPABLE OF TURNING PEOPLE'S SPUN GOODS INTO YARDS OF FABRIC FOR MILES. IN FACT, WOMEN CAME FROM 10 TO 12 MILES AWAY TO GET ME TO WEAVE THEIR SPUN GOODS INTO CLOTH. I WORKED SO HARD, MAKING SURE I WAS ALWAYS DONE AND READY WHEN I SAID I WOULD BE.

FINISHED ALREADY?!

JUST CALL ME OL' RELIABLE!

I'D LIKE YOU TO MAKE STRIPES WITH THE RED AND WHITE WOOL PLEASE.

THAT'S FINE, JUST ADD ANOTHER WEEK ONTO MY FINISH TIME.

DAVID AND I WORKED TOGETHER TO PROVIDE A LIVING. I BROUGHT IN MONEY FROM MY WEAVING, SEWING, KNITTING, BRAIDED STRAW, RAG RUGS, FRUITS, VEGETABLES, DRIED GOODS, AND SEEDS I COLLECTED FROM MY PLANTS EACH YEAR. WE WERE A TEAM AND WE NEEDED EACH OTHER.

PATTY, CAN YOU COME GIVE ME A HAND WITH THIS POST?!

*$4 would be the equivalent to about $82 in 2020.

DAVID'S MOTHER WAS A GOOD WOMAN, BUT HELPING HER AT TIMES CAME WITH ITS CHALLENGES.

*Rachel was either bedridden or confined to a wheelchair. She did pop Patty's elbow out of joint.
**Skullcap is a plant. The above ground parts are used to make medicine. Skullcap is used for many conditions, but so far, there isn't enough scientific evidence to determine whether or not it is effective for any of them. WebMD

RACHEL WAS SKILLED IN MIDWIFERY. I LEARNED MUCH FROM WATCHING HER.

RUB PEPPERMINT OIL ON HIS CHEST AND IT WILL HELP HIM BREATHE BETTER.

IS MOTHER SESSIONS HERE?! I NEED HER TO COME AND TAKE CARE OF MY WIFE AND SICK BABE!

I'LL GO GRAB YOUR SUPPLIES.

OH, YES, I'LL BE THERE FASTER THAN A JACKRABBIT CAN HOP.

HOW FAST DO JACKRABBITS HOP?!

*The town doctor did in fact see Patty's patient she had healed and sought Patty out afterwards to encourage her to become a midwife.

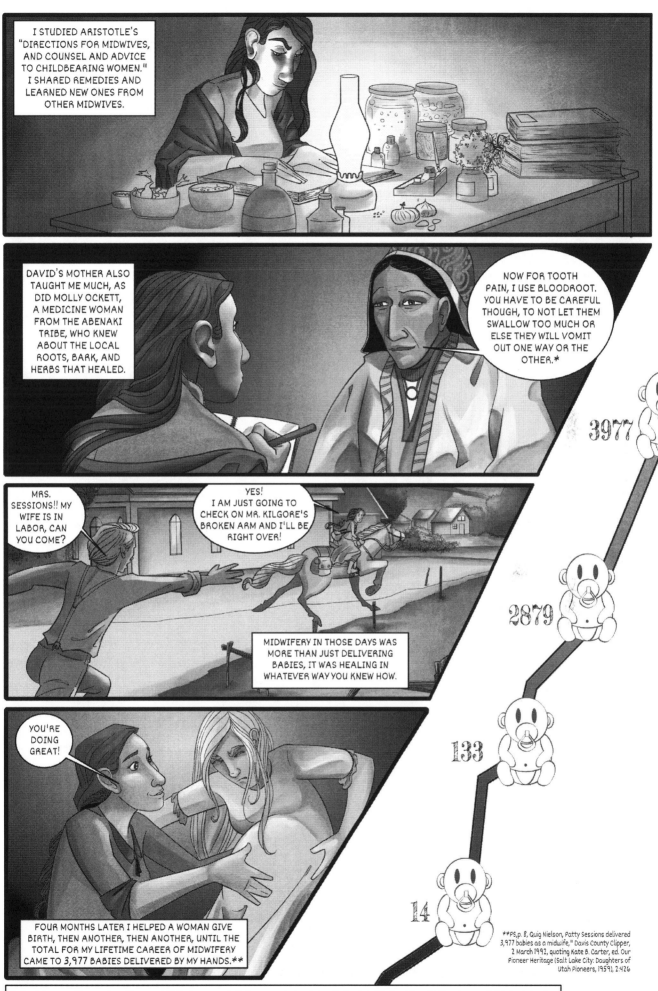

I STUDIED ARISTOTLE'S "DIRECTIONS FOR MIDWIVES, AND COUNSEL AND ADVICE TO CHILDBEARING WOMEN." I SHARED REMEDIES AND LEARNED NEW ONES FROM OTHER MIDWIVES.

DAVID'S MOTHER ALSO TAUGHT ME MUCH, AS DID MOLLY OCKETT, A MEDICINE WOMAN FROM THE ABENAKI TRIBE, WHO KNEW ABOUT THE LOCAL ROOTS, BARK, AND HERBS THAT HEALED.

NOW FOR TOOTH PAIN, I USE BLOODROOT. YOU HAVE TO BE CAREFUL THOUGH, TO NOT LET THEM SWALLOW TOO MUCH OR ELSE THEY WILL VOMIT OUT ONE WAY OR THE OTHER.*

3977

MRS. SESSIONS!! MY WIFE IS IN LABOR, CAN YOU COME?

YES! I AM JUST GOING TO CHECK ON MR. KILGORE'S BROKEN ARM AND I'LL BE RIGHT OVER!

MIDWIFERY IN THOSE DAYS WAS MORE THAN JUST DELIVERING BABIES, IT WAS HEALING IN WHATEVER WAY YOU KNEW HOW.

2879

YOU'RE DOING GREAT!

133

FOUR MONTHS LATER I HELPED A WOMAN GIVE BIRTH, THEN ANOTHER, THEN ANOTHER, UNTIL THE TOTAL FOR MY LIFETIME CAREER OF MIDWIFERY CAME TO 3,977 BABIES DELIVERED BY MY HANDS.**

14

**PS,p. 8, Quig Nielson, Patty Sessions delivered 3,977 babies as a midwife," Davis County Clipper, 2 March 1992, quoting Kate B. Carter, ed. Our Pioneer Heritage (Salt Lake City: Daughters of Utah Pioneers, 1959), 1:426

*Molly Ockett was a well known Native medicine woman/midwife who was respected by the European immigrants due to her knowledge in healing, delivery of babies and more particularly knowledge of their language and culture. Patty does not indicate in her journals that she actually learned from her, but it is very likely she could have, seeing how they traversed the same area and were contemporaries. It is even possible that Molly could have delivered Patty as a baby.

MY MEDICINAL RECIPES (that I wrote down in my journals like this) WERE TRIED AND TRUE. FOR EYE DROPS, I WRAP TWO EGGS IN A WET CLOTH AND ROAST THEM TILL THEY ARE QUITE HARD. THEN I GRATE OR POUND THEM FINE AND ADD HALF OF THE WHITE VITRIOL AND MIX IT WELL.

THEN I ADD ONE PINT OF WARM RAIN WATER AND KEEP IT WARM FOR THREE HOURS, OFTEN STIRRING OR SHAKING IT. THEN I STRAIN IT THROUGH A FINE THICK FLANNEL AND BOTTLE IT UP FOR USE.*

THIS TEAPLES EYE WATER MEDICINE I MADE SHOULD DO THE TRICK.

DROP THIS INTO YOUR EYE THREE TIMES A DAY.

SUGAR   ZINC

Ingredients:
White vitriol= zinc sulfate.
Side effects include abdominal pain, vomiting, headaches, and tiredness.

WHAT ON EARTH DID YOU DO?!

BESSY, MY COW DIED FROM SOMETHING STRANGE AND I NEEDED TO DRAG HER AWAY TO BE DISPOSED OF.

OKAY, LET ME JUST WRAP IT UP IN CATNIP, LOBELIA, THEN SOME SALT.... SOAP... AND MOLASSES AND HOPE FOR THE BEST!

Indian Hemp root: cure for gravel, for dropsy & for fits. For stifle: use the white of an egg beat to a froth. When the oil settles to the bottom, put it all on bathe it in with hot iron. ***

OPEN WIDE PETER! IT DOESN'T TASTE AS BAD AS YOU FEEL.

*Ophthalmologists today treat patients with severe ocular surface damage with amniotic membranes. Perhaps there is something to the amniotic membrane of a chicken egg that worked....even if it was hard roasted and grated? Definitely don't try this at home.
**Metallic zinc was first produced in India sometime in the 1400s by heating the mineral calamine (ZnCO3) with wool. Zinc was rediscovered by Andreas Sigismund Marggraf in 1746 by heating calamine with charcoal. Today, most zinc is produced through the electrolysis of aqueous zinc sulfate (ZnSO4). (https://education.jlab.org › itselemental › ele030).

1 oz gumgabba rum, 2 do megunda pitch) 1 lb rosin) 2 h oz hartshorn* last put in heat it together like cooking wax this for strengthening plaster. *

for salve for old sores: the bark of indigo weed root boiled down beas wax a very little rosin. *

For stifle...

...TAKE ONE TABLESPOONFUL OF CASTILE SOAP MIXED WITH SUGAR THREE MORNINGS THEN MISS THREE UNTIL IT IS TAKEN NINE MORNINGS...

...until it operates,** shure cure ***.

For vomiting: six drops laudanum the size of pea soda 2 h teaspoon peppermint 2 h tea cups water take a tablespoonful at a time till it stops it if the first dose don't repeat it.

Harts horn, laudanum, carbonate ammonia, sweet oil, camphor for milk leg or inflammation or swelling.

***These are long lost recipes for illnesses that go by different names now: Stifle- constipation would be my guess, but really no clue here. Gravel: a disease characterized by small stones which are formed in the kidneys, passed along the ureters to the bladder, and expelled with the urine. See also stranguary. Synonym: kidney stone.(https://www.thornber.net/medicine/html/medgloss.html) PS,p. Dropsy was an old term used to describe edema, or excess water in the body. This condition may have been associated with people experiencing congestive heart failure. The blood is not getting enough oxygen and nutrients. Modern treatment includes a change in diet to reduce salt and cholesterol.
*These are recipes straight from Patty's journal, as she wrote them. Sound confusing? Yes, to us, but it wasn't to her!
**"Until it operates" probably meant, until you can poo!
***Patty spelled phonetically and changed the way she spelled words often.

*Lobelia= Indian tobacco; used for cardiovascular diseases, but it is now considered poisonous. It is similar to nicotine. Dangerous to children and pregnant women and people with cardiac diseases. Excessive use will cause nausea and vomiting.Prior to rescue inhalers around the 1950's, lobelia was used as a treatment for bronchial asthma and in Patty's situations; whooping cough, cold, flu, most any ailment.
**This didn't happen, however, Patty was asked to lay hands on and heal Mary Ann Nobles who was not well. Mary Ann told Patty that she had spoken to Sarah Nobles, who had been dead for over two years and talked with her for over one hour. PS,p. 132.

HERE YOU ARE! A SWEET BABY GIRL.

UM...MRS. SESSIONS, DO YOU MIND CHECKING ON MY 2 SICK HORSES AS WELL?*

MY LIFE AT THIS POINT STARTED BEING FILLED WITH BABIES. MY BABIES BEING BORN AND PASSING AWAY AND OTHER WOMEN'S BABIES THAT I HELPED BRING INTO THE WORLD AND ALSO BURY.

* Charles Stodard actually brought his horses to Patty in Salt Lake City Utah, but for the sake of storytelling has been added here. PS.p.279

DAVID AND I EVENTUALLY OWNED 400 ACRES OF LAND THAT WE FARMED. HE BUILT US A LARGE HOUSE, TWO BARNS, A SAW MILL, A GRIST MILL (TO GRIND GRAIN), AND SEVERAL SHEDS. WE WERE SET.

THAT IS UNTIL I DECIDED TO UPROOT OUR FAMILY AND HEAD WEST.

PERRIGRINE, WHAT DO YOU THINK THOSE MEN WANT?

THE YEARS PAST AND MY CHILDREN WERE OLDER NOW. PERRIGRINE WAS MARRIED WITH ONE CHILD.

"CHRIST VISITED "OTHER SHEEP" WHICH WERE NOT OF THE FOLD IN JERUSALEM AND THEY'RE RECORDED IN WHAT IS CALLED "THE BOOK OF MORMON" ABOUT THE LANDS IN THE AMERICAS."

"SHEEP? WHY ARE THEY TALKING ABOUT BAPTIZING SHEEP?"

* In the span of 8 years Patty lost 7 people in her life, which included children and parents. Patty buried four of her eight kids in Maine. Women's Exponent issues: 13 (September 1,1884) 51:13 (September 15, 1884): 63;13 (November 1, 1884):86;13 (November 15, 1884): 94-95;13 (February 1, 1885): 134-35; 13 (March1, 1885): 150-51;14 (June 1, 1885):2,14 (November 15, 1885):85-86,94-95.   *The world infant mortality rates in the 1800s was 43.3% compared with 3.4% today.(ourworlddata.org)

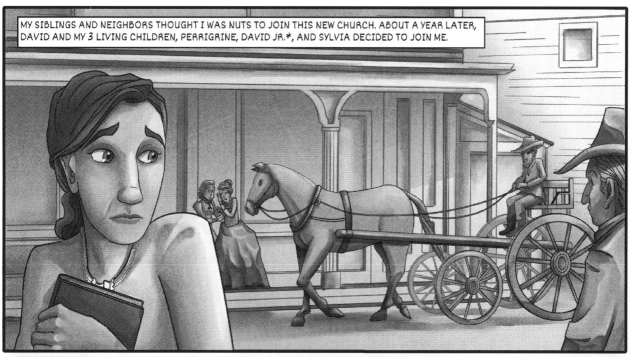

MY SIBLINGS AND NEIGHBORS THOUGHT I WAS NUTS TO JOIN THIS NEW CHURCH. ABOUT A YEAR LATER, DAVID AND MY 3 LIVING CHILDREN, PERRIGRINE, DAVID JR.*, AND SYLVIA DECIDED TO JOIN ME.

I KNOW WE'VE ONLY BEEN A PART OF THIS CHURCH A FEW YEARS, BUT EVERYONE HATES THE MORMONS** SO MUCH THAT WE NEED TO MOVE WITH THE OTHERS TO BE A UNIFIED GROUP IN OHIO.

DAD, TIMES ARE HARD AND MONEY IS SCARCE ANYWAY. LET'S JUST SELL OFF THE PROPERTY AND START A NEW LIFE ALL TOGETHER.

BY THE WAY, I AM GOING TO HAVE ANOTHER BABY! BUT THAT WON'T HINDER THE MOVE, SO LET'S GET ON WITH IT!

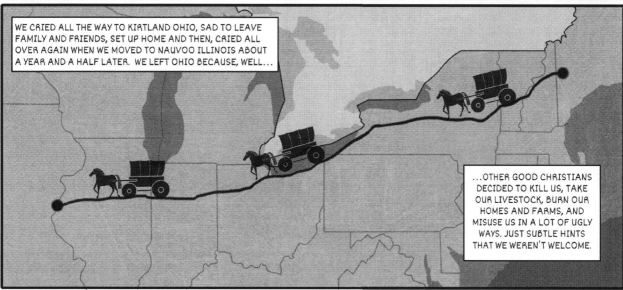

WE CRIED ALL THE WAY TO KIRTLAND OHIO, SAD TO LEAVE FAMILY AND FRIENDS, SET UP HOME AND THEN, CRIED ALL OVER AGAIN WHEN WE MOVED TO NAUVOO ILLINOIS ABOUT A YEAR AND A HALF LATER. WE LEFT OHIO BECAUSE, WELL...

...OTHER GOOD CHRISTIANS DECIDED TO KILL US, TAKE OUR LIVESTOCK, BURN OUR HOMES AND FARMS, AND MISUSE US IN A LOT OF UGLY WAYS. JUST SUBTLE HINTS THAT WE WEREN'T WELCOME.

*Patty's son David is actually David the 4th.
**The Mormon church is really called 'The Church of Jesus Christ of Latter Day Saints'. However, that name is such a mouthful, that people, including the members themselves refer to the Church as the "Mormon church". Named after the man Mormon (circa 400 AD) who chiseled his record into gold plates, the ones Joseph Smith translated.
***Multiple reason went into the members needing to flee for their lives. Some reasons being consequence of angry dissenters from the church causing uproar, warranted or not. The members of the church were the recipients of murder, rape, and plunder of home and properties.

FEBRUARY 1839

AT LEAST WE DIDN'T PUT THE WOOD FLOORS IN YET..

MANY NEW CONVERTS UNDERSTANDABLY HAD ENOUGH AND GAVE UP ON THIS NEW RELIGION. PROFESSING A NEW VIEW OF GOD AND PUTTING YOUR FAITH IN HUMAN PROPHETS TO LEAD YOU RIGHT, WAS A LOT TO GO THROUGH.

WHAT DO YOU MEAN YOU CAN'T GIVE ME MY MONEY?! (*)

I, HOWEVER, WAS TOTALLY EMPOWERED BY THIS RELIGION, DESPITE THE MANY HUMAN FAILINGS I WITNESSED.

WELL, KICKING THE MORMONS OUT WAS THE EASIEST WAY TO GET LAND!

YAH, WE HAVE OUR PICK OF FULLY FURNISHED HOMES AND PRE-PLOWED FIELDS READY FOR SPRING PLANTING.

I CAN'T DO THIS... THIS IS TOO HARD. WHY AM I DOING THIS?

I CAN DO THIS! I BELIEVE IN THIS! THIS IS WORTH IT!

*Kirtland Safety Society bank failed due to limited reserve. That's the short and sweet of it. For longer, not sweet details you would need to read other sources on the matter.

WE SETTLED IN NAUVOO, ILLINOIS IN TIME FOR ME TO BURY MY EIGHTH CHILD.

The baby was born four days later, small in size, thought to be premature. The husband later sued the doctor for the pain and damages he caused to his wife. Patty had to testify in court to what she witnessed. The husband received a refund of his payment to the doctor as damages. (Joseph Smith History, 1838-1856, vol.D-1)

NAUVOO BECAME A LARGE CITY FAST AND WAS BIGGER THAN THE CITY OF CHICAGO AT THE TIME. MANY CONVERTS MOVED FROM EUROPE TO JOIN US. IT MADE FOR INTERESTING CONVERSATIONS.

HELO, BRAF CWRDD Â CHI.

HALLO, FREUT MICH, DICH KENNENZULERNEN

HELLO, NICE TO MEET YOU.

HEJ, DEJLIGT AT MØDE DIG.

I BECAME VERY GOOD FRIENDS WITH ELIZA ROXCY SNOW AND ZINA HUNTINGTON YOUNG AS WELL AS OTHER WIVES OF THE APOSTLES. I WAS A PART OF SPECIAL GROUP OF POWERFUL AND INFLUENTIAL WOMEN.(*)

PATTY WE'VE BEEN ASKED TO GO HEAL A SICK BROTHER.

DON'T LET ME FORGET TO GIVE YOU MY FROG SOUP RECIPE, IT WORKS WONDERS FOR NEW MOTHERS.

WE LOVED TO HOLD OUR OWN PRIVATE MEETINGS TOGETHER WHERE WE BLESSED EACH OTHER, ATE, DRANK, AND SPOKE IN TONGUES. WE THRIVED ON THIS KIND OF WORSHIP AND CAMARADERIE. WE WERE HEALERS PHYSICALLY, SPIRITUALLY, AND AS BEST WE COULD - SCIENTIFICALLY.

SERI VADA VELLIE....

PATTY SAYS THAT....(**)

(*)Eliza Roxcy Snow, a poet, 2nd general President of the women's organization, the "Relief Society", women's suffrage advocate and friends to Susan B. Anthony, also designed and developed one of the first women's pant suits (too early for it's time to catch on). Zina Huntington Young, also a midwife, 3rd President of the Women's Relief Society, and valuable women's suffrage advocate and also friend to Susan B. Anthony.
(**)Speaking in tongues according to early members of the church, is where a person speaks (what was thought to be the Adamic Language, or language Adam and Eve first spoke, or what we spoke in Heaven), while someone else interprets. If there was not an interpreter, then it was not thought to be from God. Current members do not practice this, and would view it as extremely odd if someone did.

DURING THE NAUVOO YEARS, I HAD MY SALVATION SECURED BY BEING "SEALED" OR MARRIED BY THE POWER OF HEAVEN TO JOSEPH SMITH, AS WAS MY DAUGHTER SYLVIA...

...AND FOR THAT MATTER QUITE A FEW OTHER WOMEN. JOSEPH, IN HIS PROPOSALS TO WOMEN, WOULD TELL THEM THAT HE WAS THEIR MEANS OF GETTING TO HEAVEN.(*)

AND NOW I PRONOUNCE YOU MAN AND WIFE, AND WIFE, AND WIFE, AND WIFE...

OUR WOMEN'S RELIEF SOCIETY MEETINGS WERE A LITTLE AWKWARD NOW AND THEN.(*)

DO ANY OF YOU KNOW WHERE JOSEPH IS? I HAVE A FEELING I SHOULDN'T BE SO TRUSTING.

OUR TIME IN NAUVOO WAS WONDERFUL AND AWFUL. WE WORKED REALLY HARD TO BUILD UP OUR CITY AND OUR RELIGION. AT THE SAME TIME, OUR LEADER WAS IN AND OUT OF HIDING QUITE A BIT BECAUSE HE PROFESSED TO HAVE SEEN GOD AND CHRIST AS TWO DIFFERENT BEINGS, PREACHED ADDITIONAL SCRIPTURES AND TAUGHT PLURAL MARRIAGE.

IT CAUSED A LOT OF CONFUSION AMONG OUR PEOPLE AND TO PEOPLE OUTSIDE OF OUR GROUP. IT EVENTUALLY LED TO JOSEPH'S AND HIS BROTHER'S MURDERS.

(*)Yes, this would be considered polyandry, when one female marries more than one male. Confused? Join the club. PS,p. 277
(**)This may be one of the most troubling times in the church's history. Joseph Smith introduced the concept/ theology of polygamy. As he did, he secretly married many women at first unbeknownst to his wife Emma, then to her knowledge. She didn't accept it at first, then grudgingly accepted, and then totally denied its existence in what may have been her way of coping with her world falling apart around her. Emma said that, "Joseph ruined a beautiful religion" but she never denied that her husband was a Prophet of God and firmly believed he translated the Book of Mormon from real ancient texts on gold plates. Emma's frustrations can be read throughout the Relief Society Minutes found online in the Joseph Smith Papers web link. *Mormon Enigma; Linda King Newell and Valeen Tippetts Avery.* Nauvoo Relief Society Minute Bookpg 17. Women's Relief Society was first established in Nauvoo in an effort to perform services for the community. Emma voted as President. (***)*Many things led up the murder of Joseph and his brother Hyrum. The members in Nauvoo were increasing and Joseph's political power because of them felt threatening to outsiders. Joseph was in and out of prisons even before he starting teaching and practicing polygamy. The anger and hatred outsiders felt towards this group of people is quite remarkable and inhumane, despite the part members may have played in its initial cause.

FEBRUARY 1846

THE VIOLENCE SPREAD AND PEOPLE ONCE AGAIN STARTED KILLING US AND TOOK OVER OUR PROPERTY. THEY WERE AFRAID AND DISTURBED BY US. SO MOST OF US LEFT AND STARTED THE COLD, LONG, HARD TREK TO THE UNKNOWN. WHICH LATER BECAME UTAH.

OH BOY...

HERE WE GO!

WHAT AM I DOING?

PATTY, WE NEED TO MAKE ROOM FOR ROSILLA'S THINGS. I MARRIED HER THIS AFTERNOON.

YEAH WELL, I THINK IT'S OKAY THAT I GOT SEALED TO JOSEPH, BUT THIS IS DIFFERENT, I DON'T LIKE THIS ONE BIT.

PERRIGRINE, MAKE SURE ROSILLA IS CARED FOR TILL SHE IS READY TO COME WITH YOUR GROUP AND CATCH UP WITH US. *

WE WILL, SEE YOU IN A FEW MONTHS!

* David married Rosilla before they left Nauvoo. Rosilla did not join them right away, but was brought by Perrigrine later. PS, p. 24.

I BET I COVERED DOUBLE THE GROUND OTHERS WALKED BECAUSE I RODE OR WALKED BACK AND FORTH DELIVERING BABIES IN FRONT OF THE WAGON TRAIN OR BEHIND THE WAGON TRAIN.
IT TOOK MONTHS AND A LITTLE LAYOVER AT AN ENCAMPMENT, "WINTER QUARTERS" IN NEBRASKA.

*PS,p.54 Patty notes that she, "put black Jane to bed with a son." Jane Manning James, a free Black woman, joined with her mother and siblings, the church in Connecticut and with them, traveled by foot to Nauvoo, Illinois to be with the other members. Jane and her family, according to her own record, were very welcomed, loved, and involved in the community.
**Isaac James, a free Black man who met Jane in Nauvoo.

SHE'S JUST ABOUT TWO MILES BACK!

I FOUND THIS OL' CABIN AS SHELTER...

WELL, BABY DIDN'T WAIT FOR US. STILL PLENTY FOR ME TO DO.

THERE WERE ALWAYS THINGS TO ATTEND TO EVEN AFTER THE BABY WAS BORN.

THERE WAS THE AFTERBIRTH THAT NEEDED TO COME AS WELL AS MAKE SURE THE MOTHER AND BABY WERE IN GOOD CONDITION. *

*PS, p.41 : afterbirth=placenta that comes out after the baby is born.

*PS,p. 44: Jane Glenn born 1805, just 10 years younger than Patty.
**Brigham Young was the Prophet and leader after Joseph Smith's death.

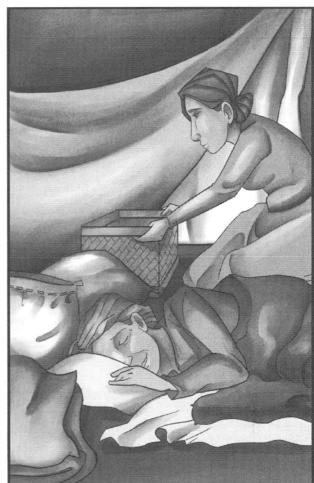

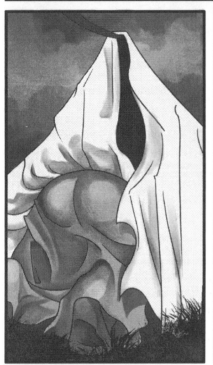

*PS, p.57 "I slept alone"

*The rain after the war dance was pure coincidence. The Natives recorded in Patty's journal were there to celebrate the 4th of July, or rather to show good will to the pioneers on their holiday as they passed through the Native's land.

AS WE TRAVELED ALONG IN ALL KINDS OF WEATHER, MY BODY WAS BEATEN DOWN AND WEARY. WE HAD LITTLE FOOD, AND BLANKETS THAT NEVER HAD TIME TO DRY. I FELT SICK ALL THE TIME, BUT CONTINUED TO DELIVER BABY AFTER BABY, DAY AFTER DAY AND WATCHED MY DAVID DRIFT AWAY.

ROSILLA, PATTY, THERE ARE GRAPES OVER THE RIVER READY FOR THE PICKIN'!

I WAS SO FULL OF GRIEF THAT THERE WAS NO ROOM FOR FOOD. *

*...and I soon threw it up. PSp.58 direct quote

I KEPT A CAREFUL RECORD OF EVERY SINGLE PERSON I HELPED, LIVING OR NOT.

Sunday 3:
Sam Thomas died last night.

Thunder storm, wind and rain blew many trees down. Some fell on the horses and cattle.

Wednesday 6:
Sister Lathrop sent for me. she was very sick.

Saturday 9:
Hosea Stout's child died with the fits. I went and laid it out.

None killed. Several horses bit by snakes.

THE WAGON TRAIN MOVED SLOWLY AS LIFE PASSED QUICKLY BY.

*https://en.wikipedia.org/wiki/Winter_Quarters_(North_Omaha,_Nebraska).
**Perrigrine in his journal states that they built around 1200 houses.PS,p66 (DPG,pp B-46-47).

ROSILLA NEVER HELPED. SHE DID NOT LIKE SHARING A HUSBAND OR THE "HOUSEHOLD" DUTIES.

I DIDN'T LIKE SHARING MY HUSBAND EITHER AND HAD TO PUT UP WITH ROSILLA FILLING DAVID'S HEAD WITH LIES ABOUT ME AND HOW I TREATED HER.

HE MADE ME FEEL AS THOUGH MY HEART WOULD BURST WITH SADNESS.

SHE MAKES ME DO ALL THE COOKING AND WASHING AND SHE MAKES ME MASSAGE HER FEET WHEN YOU'RE NOT LOOKING AND SHE PUTS SAND IN MY MUSH...*

I'LL LEAVE YOU PATTY IF YOU DON'T CHANGE AND BECOME A BETTER WIFE!

DAVID AND ROSILLA'S TREATMENT OF ME MADE ME SICK. NO REALLY, I BECAME SO LITERALLY ILL THAT ONE OF THE CAMP DOCTORS SAID TO PREPARE FOR MY DEATH.

SHE HAS INFLAMMATION OF THE STOMACH.

IT WILL BE A MIRACLE IF SHE GETS BETTER.

*We don't know what Rosilla actually said to David, but Patty records in her journals that she did turn David against her. David constantly spoke so harshly to Patty about it that Patty became ill enough to almost die. She gave up wanting to live, but her close friends wouldn't let her.

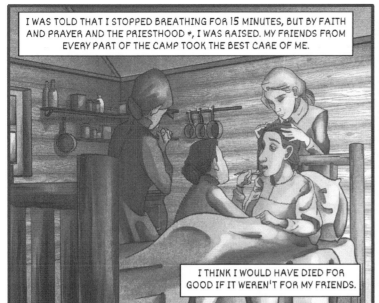

I WAS TOLD THAT I STOPPED BREATHING FOR 15 MINUTES, BUT BY FAITH AND PRAYER AND THE PRIESTHOOD *, I WAS RAISED. MY FRIENDS FROM EVERY PART OF THE CAMP TOOK THE BEST CARE OF ME.

I THINK I WOULD HAVE DIED FOR GOOD IF IT WEREN'T FOR MY FRIENDS.

BRIGHAM AND HEBER ** LAID HANDS ON MY HEAD TO BLESS ME.

PATTY, WE BLESS YOUR BODY TO HEAL.

ROSILLA, HOLD YOUR TONGUE OR I'LL ROLL THE WAGON AWAY WITH YOU IN IT!***

YOU TWO ALMOST KILLED HER WITH YOUR LIES AND ABUSING WORDS!

DID YOU KNOW I DELIVERED ARTEMESIA BEAMAN'S BABE AND SHE NAMED HIM MAHONRI MORIANCUMER? ****

IS THAT SO??

AM I THE ONLY ONE TO EXPERIENCE SUCH PAIN??!!!

YOUR BABY WILL BE THE THIRD BIRTH I'VE ATTENDED TODAY.

SOON ENOUGH, LIFE WENT BACK TO NORMAL.

THIS IS MY 20TH CHILD I HAVE BIRTHED.

SORT OF...

*"Though the spiritual occasions when the sisters met to strengthen each other took on a celebratory air, there was no hint of usurping or infringing on male priesthood authority. The women merely exercised the spiritual gifts and powers to which they knew they were entitled. The men also recognized, approved of, and sometimes participated in, and encouraged the women's activities." Patty wrote on 22 November 1847, in the evening prayed for Heber Kimball with Ellen and Mary Ellen Kimball's wives. I anointed Ellen according to Heber's request when he met me on the road." *Mormon Midwife The 1846-1888 Diaries of Patty Bartlett Sessions*, Donna Toland Smart, page 28.
**Patty refers to President Brigham Young and Apostles Heber C. Kimball in such a familiar way as, Brigham and Heber. She refers to her own husband as "Mr. Sessions" not David. P.S. p.60.
***Peregrine really told Rosilla that he would roll her away in the wagon.
****"Monday 4 put Erastus Snow's wife Artemesia Beaman to bed with a son Mahonri Moriancumer. P.S. p.69.

AS THE MONTHS FLEW BY, I CONTINUED TO DELIVER BABY AFTER BABY AND MAKE AND GIVE MEDICINE TO THE SICK. ROSILLA CONTINUED TO STAND BY AND WATCH AS I COOKED, WASHED, AND TOOK CARE OF EVERYTHING. DAVID TOOK TURNS SPEAKING HARSHLY TO EACH OF US DEPENDING ON WHO HE BELIEVED FOR THE DAY.

BY DECEMBER, ROSILLA THANKFULLY HAD ENOUGH OF IT ALL AND JOINED OTHERS TO HEAD BACK OVER THE MISSISSIPPI RIVER. I CAN'T SAY THAT I WAS ONE BIT SAD ABOUT IT.*

I AM SO SORRY, I PROMISE NEVER TO TREAT YOU SO POORLY AGAIN.

LIFE BECAME MORE NORMAL, FOOD MORE AVAILABLE, AND THE BABIES KEPT POURING IN.

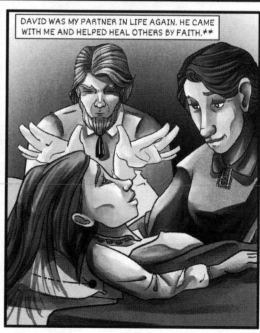

DAVID WAS MY PARTNER IN LIFE AGAIN. HE CAME WITH ME AND HELPED HEAL OTHERS BY FAITH.**

*Rosilla did not continue with the church members and went back to Illinois. As aggravating as she was to Patty, how odd it must have been to be a young wife in the mix of an older couple's marriage.
**PS, Patty and David blessing others p.75,77,78.

BY JUNE 1847, WE WERE READY TO HEAD OUT AGAIN IN SEARCH OF OUR LAND. A LAND WHERE WE COULD BE LEFT ALONE. BEFORE PACKING UP THOUGH, I MET WITH MY FRIENDS AND WE BLESSED EACH OTHER FOR OUR JOURNEY.

PATTY, YOU WILL BE BLESSED BY MANY AS YOU BLESS OTHERS. THEY WILL RISE UP AND SAY THAT YOUR HANDS WERE THE FIRST THAT HANDLED THEM AND THEN THEIR MOTHERS WILL RISE UP AND BLESS YOU.

FINALLY! SOON WE CAN BUILD A HOME AND HAVE A NORMAL LIFE AGAIN!

THE BABIES HOWEVER, DID NOT CARE THAT WE WERE BUSY TRAVELING HARSH ROADS ONCE MORE.

WHICH WAGON IS SHE IN?

THEY KEPT COMING AND I KEPT DELIVERING THEM.

AoOo owWW!!

*Friday 30 go 20 miles pass the chimney rock and many places looked like ancient buildings. Camp on the river and find good feed. Kill a rattlesnake, save the gall and grease. PS,p. 93-94.
**Snake venom was used for "chronic nervous palpitations of the heart, depression, anxiety attacks... (*Animal Simples, Approved for Modern Uses and Cures.* William Thomas Fernie.pg 457).

THIS IS THE PLACE, RIDE ON!*

Winter Quarters

Nebraska

Nauvoo

Salt Lake Utah

Illinois

SEPTEMBER 18 1847

AUGUST 22 1847

JULY 15 1847

JULY 03 1847

JUNE 11 1847

*Brigham actually came and said this in his first entrance into Utah on July 24, 1847. He then came back with Patty's group to show them where to go.

*Lorenzo Dow Jr., son of Harriet P. Wheeler and Lorenzo Young was born on September 26, 1847. Patty was told five months prior that her "hands [would] be the first to handle the first born son in the place of rest for the saints even in the city of our God. I have come more than one thousand miles to do it since it was spoken." PS, p.99.

The trek was grueling, clothes impractical, food sparse, but the views...

...oh the views!

DAVID AND I GOT TO WORK BUILDING OUR NEW HOME IN WHAT WOULD BECOME DOWNTOWN SALT LAKE CITY.

WE WORKED HARD TO SET UP LIFE FOR THE FOURTH TIME SINCE LEAVING MAINE.

MY OLDEST, PERRIGRINE SETTLED IN WHAT BECAME KNOWN AS THE CITY OF BOUNTIFUL.

SISTER SESSIONS.... BROTHER SESSIONS, CAN YOU COME AND HEAL MY WIFE?

SURE BROTHER SNOW.

I TOOK CARE OF SISTER SNOW'S MEDICAL NEEDS AND DAVID HELPED ME BLESS HER AFTERWARD. *

PATTY, I WAS JUST COMING TO GET YOU.

CAN YOU COME ANOINT AND HEAL MY WIFE ELLEN?

OF COURSE BROTHER KIMBALL. **

*It seems that the pioneers were more practical in their approach to religion at times. Husbands and wives could act more as a team when asked to give blessings. Mothers and fathers blessing their own children. In the church today, one has to call around to different households to find two men to give a blessing. Sister Snow was blessed by Patty and David in April 1848.

** PS, p.103 Heber C. Kimball, was a member of the Twelve Apostles, a high figure within the patriarchy, making it all the more interesting that he is asking Patty to heal, when one would assume he would be the man for the job.

BEING CALLED OUT TO DELIVER BABIES AT ALL TIMES, DAY OR NIGHT, CAUSED ME TO STUMBLE UPON INTERESTING HAPPENINGS IN THE COMMUNITY.*

WHAT THE .....?!

THAT SIMEON CARTER TREATING HIS WIFE LYDIA THAT WAY!!OOOOH.

I TOOK CAREFUL NOTE OF WHO I SAW.

TOM GATES AND SAM LANCE! WHAT ARE YOU OLD FOOLS UP TO?!

OH OOOH, I SHOULD HAVE KNOWN PATTY WOULD BE UP.

*Mormon Midwife The 1846-1888 Diaries of Patty Bartlett Sessions, Donna Toland Smart: pg 139-140.Patty later was a witness to "examine" and find Sister Carter "innocent". We have to draw our own conclusions here, but it seems Simeon should have been the one "on trial". It is also interesting to note that he took in another plural wife nine days after Patty saw him pushing his first wife into the mud.
** PS,p. 134

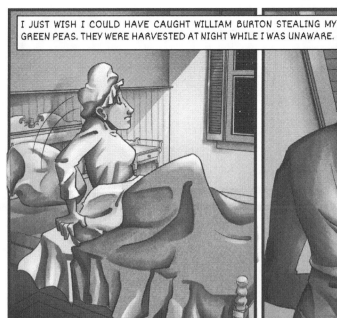

I JUST WISH I COULD HAVE CAUGHT WILLIAM BURTON STEALING MY GREEN PEAS. THEY WERE HARVESTED AT NIGHT WHILE I WAS UNAWARE.

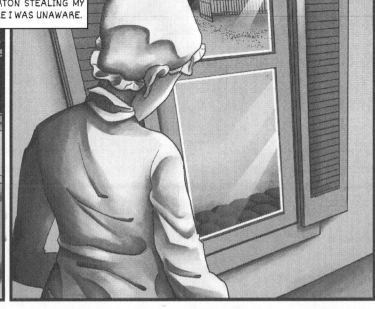

I FOLLOWED THE TRAIL OF PEAS THE CULPRIT LEFT BEHIND, RIGHT UP TO WILLIAM'S WAGON.

YOU OL' RASCAL!

HE, OF COURSE, HAD TAKEN MY PEAS TO TRADE WITH THE INCOMING IMMIGRANTS.*

*There were many different times when people came knocking on Patty's door for help. She notes on June 26, 1856 that, "I have so many here to buy flour and I have so little to spare I hardly know who needs it most for they all tell the same story and it almost makes me sick because I cannot supply their wants..." PS,p.234.

**In 1882 Priddy Meeks wrote about the famine caused by crickets and other misfortunes and his wife's interaction with Patty in trying to obtain flour. The wife does not mention David in her account to her husband, but I have added him to perhaps explain why Patty kept upping the price on the woman. ("Journal," p. 20, typescript, Utah State Historical Society, Salt Lake City)PS p. 116 footnote.   *David was able to get 50 cents per pound of flour from the mill when times were good. PS,p.148.

IN BETWEEN THE BUSYNESS OF MY LIFE I DID INDULGE IN OTHER ACTIVITIES SUCH AS GETTING MY FORTUNE TOLD BY SISTER HATCH.*

IT LOOKS LIKE YOU WILL LOSE MONEY, BUT THEN FIND IT AFTER A LONG SEARCH.

YOU WILL FEEL TROUBLED, BUT THEN BE GLAD TO SEE A MAN YOU HAVEN'T SEEN IN A LONG TIME.

YOUR HUSBAND WILL GET SICK, AND THEN GET BETTER.

I DON'T THINK I AM GOING TO COME OUT OF THIS ONE ALIVE. YOU'RE GOING TO HAVE TO TAKE CARE OF HARRIET AND HER TWO KIDS.

I SUPPORT ALL OF YOU ANYWAY.

WELL, YES.

I WILL SUPPORT HER AS LONG AS SHE LIVES IN THIS HOUSE.

BUT I CAN NOT SUPPORT HER IN ANOTHER HOME.

BECAUSE IT WILL STRETCH ME FURTHER THAN I AM ABLE.

OKAY ...AKHAK... EHHHH.

WELL THOSE CARDS WEREN'T EXACTLY CORRECT.

PATTY, I DON'T WANT TO LIVE WITH YOU.

WELL HARRIET, THEN SWEAR BEFORE THESE PEOPLE THAT YOU HAVE WILLFULLY REFUSED MY SUPPORT.

AND THAT YOU WERE WELL TAKEN CARE OF.

I WILL NOT SUPPORT YOU ANYWHERE ELSE. **

*PS, p.154 March 5, 1850 entry : Card reading or fortune telling of any kind is discouraged in the church. One's patriarchal blessing is similar, but considered the proper way to practice such curiosities.
**PS, p.151-152

*Both Patty and David tried to be true to the doctrines and commands of their religion, even at the expense of their relationship.
** PS, p. 154.

I BUILT UP AND RAN A TREE NURSERY FROM MY LAND AND SOLD TREES AND FRUIT.

I'D LIKE 50 PEACH TREES SISTER SESSIONS. *

I'D WATCH OVER MY GARDEN AT NIGHT WITH AN EAGLE EYE TO MAKE SURE NO ONE STOLE ANYTHING!**

I WAS A DUTIFUL CHURCH MEMBER AND ALWAYS PAID MY TITHING..***

I ALSO MADE MONEY FROM OUR MEN RETURNING FROM SAN DIEGO. THEY WERE PART OF OR HAD RETIRED FROM THE MORMON BATTALION AND NEEDED ROOM AND BOARD.****

TITHING OFFICE

*People bought in large quantities and Patty had raised enough to supply the demand. This is an actual amount recorded from her journal. **Patty's own words. ***Members pay ten percent of what they own, so if Patty paid 80 peach and 10 plum trees, that probably meant that she originally had 800 peach trees and 100 plum trees at home before she paid her tithe. **** The Mormon Battalion, the only religion-based unit in United States military history, served from July 1846 - July 1847 during the Mexican-American War of 1846-1848. The battalion was a volunteer unit of between 534 and 559 Latter-day Saint men, led by Mormon company officers commanded by regular U.S. Army officers. During its service, the battalion made a grueling march of nearly 2,000 miles from Council Bluffs, Iowa, to San Diego, California.

The battalion's march and service supported the eventual cession of much of the American Southwest from Mexico to the United States, especially the Gadsden Purchase of 1853 of southern Arizona and New Mexico. The march also opened a southern wagon route to California. Veterans of the battalion played significant roles in America's westward expansion in California, Utah, Arizona and other parts of the West. (*https://en.wikipedia.org/wiki/Mormon_Battalion)

**Patty was actually well off financially, but indeed said this after finding lice or some sort of bug in the bed after her guest left.

(*)Green accountant's visors were not invented until the 1900s. Just wanted to make sure you knew, I knew.

JOHN CREATED A CHOIR OF WELSH CONVERTS THAT LATER BECAME KNOWN AS THE MORMON TABERNACLE CHOIR. ONE OF UTAH'S HOTTEST SIGNING GROUPS.**

I WAS SO HAPPY. NO MORE MOVING OR RATHER BEING CHASED TO MOVE. I HAD LAND AND A HOME. I HAD GOOD FRIENDS ALL AROUND ME WHO HAD SHARED IN SUFFERING AND NOW SHARED IN THE JOY OF A SETTLED LIFE. NOTHING COULD HINDER MY HAPPINESS. AT LEAST FOR A WHILE.

* Also Patty's own words.
**Now referred to as "The Tabernacle Choir at Temple Square".

*Eliza's pant suit can be found in the pink Brigham Young home located at the 'This is the Place 'Museum.
**It was called the Council of Health.
***Emetic functions as what we know today to be similar to ipecac. Which indeed causes vomiting. Willard Richards (June 24, 1804 - March 11, 1854) was a physician and midwife/nurse trainer and an early leader in the Latter Day Saint movement. He served as Second Counselor to church president Brigham Young in the First Presidency of The Church of Jesus Christ of Latter-day Saints from 1847 until his death.

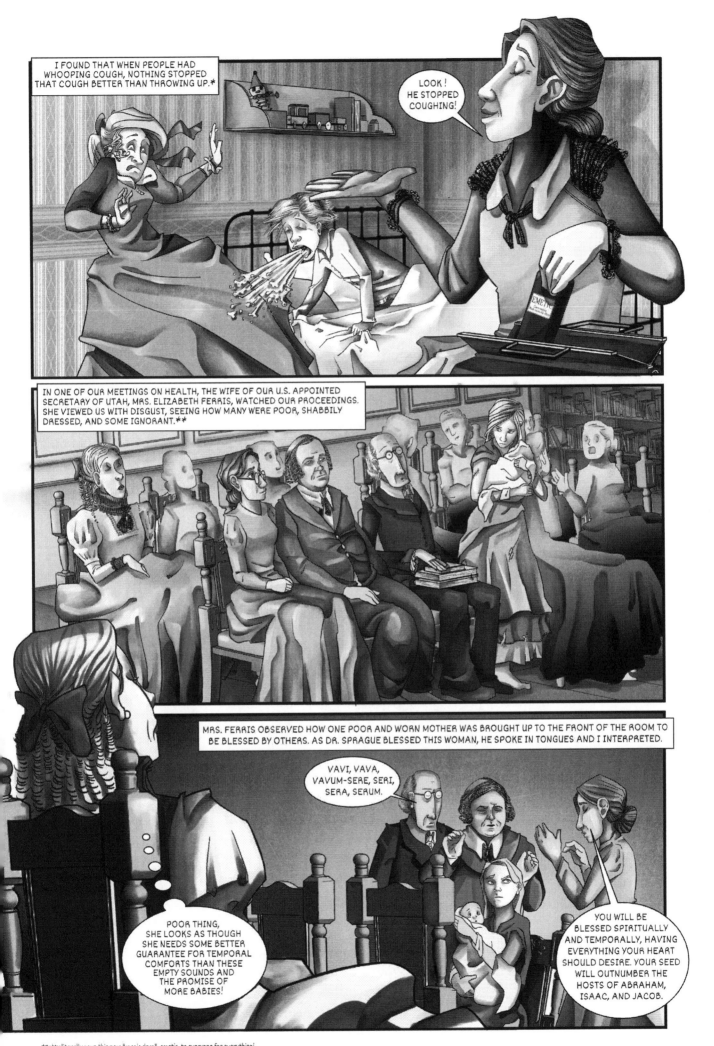

*Patty literally gave this new "magic drug", emetic, to everyone for everything!
** Elizabeth Ferris with her husband Benjamin, secretary of the Territory of Utah, visited and each wrote a book of their experiences. Mormons at Home New York:AMS Press, n.d.], 199-204; also quoted in Mormon Midwife The 1846-1888 Diaries of Patty Bartlett Sessions, Donna Toland Smart: pg 175

I RODE TWELVE MILES AND PUT SISTER SMOOT TO BED WITH A BABY, FINE BOY.

IT WAS WORTH IT, WASN'T IT?

THEN I RODE SIX MILES TO PUT SISTER JORDAN TO BED WITH A GIRL.

HERE'S THE REWARD AFTER THE PAIN.

SISTER SESSIONS, I DON'T KNOW WHAT TO DO, I NEED YOUR HELP WITH SISTER RHODES'S DELIVERY.

OKAY SUSANNAH, LETS GO!

SISTER RHODES, I THINK WE NEED TO BRING IN A DOCTOR.

NO! I'VE BEEN BUTCHERED BY DOCTORS BEFORE.

WE NEED SISTER SHEARER TO COME HELP AS WELL!

I MANAGED MANY TOUGH DELIVERY CASES, BUT ONE THAT STICKS OUT AS THE MOST DIFFICULT WAS SISTER RHODES. I MANAGED HER DELIVERY WITH TWO OTHER WOMEN AND TRIED TO CALL A DOCTOR IN, BUT SHE WOULDN'T HAVE IT.

I TRIED TO GIVE HER LOBELIA, BUT SHE WOULD NOT TAKE IT. THE BABIES ARM WAS BORN FIRST, BUT WE COULD NOT HELP HER PROGRESS BEYOND THAT.

WE BECAME SO WORRIED THAT WE FINALLY SENT FOR ELDERS AND THE DOCTOR THIS TIME. ONE DOCTOR WAS SICK AND THE OTHER DIDN'T ARRIVE TILL AFTER SISTER RHODES AND THE BABY HAD PASSED. *

HOW ABOUT TAKING SOME OF THIS, IT'LL SOOTHE YOUR NERVES...

NO!

NO BLAME WAS PLACED ON US MIDWIVES, BUT ONE OF THE DOCTORS LATER INSTRUCTED US ON HOW TO TURN BABIES IN THE WOMB WHEN THEY WEREN'T IN THE RIGHT BIRTHING POSITION. **

*Wilford Woodruff and Willard Richards came to try and heal sister Rhodes with a blessing..
**The baby was surgically removed after Sister Rhodes death. They found that the baby was laying sideways against the opening and had ruptured the womb causing the mother's death. A Dr. Andrews, who had performed the surgical removal of the dead baby, instructed the midwives on different ways to turn the baby when it was in impossible birthing positions. PS, p. 189-190.

OUR RELATIONSHIP WITH THE NATIVES IN THE LAND WAS COMPLICATED. WE BELIEVED THEY WERE DESCENDANTS OF THE PEOPLE OF THE BOOK OF MORMON WHO WERE CHILDREN OF ISRAEL - MAKING THEM OUR FAMILY AND PART OF GOD'S CHOSEN PEOPLE, WHICH MADE US DUTY BOUND IN OUR RELIGION TO CONVERT THEM AND INCLUDE THEM IN A WAY. HOWEVER, THEIR POVERTY, AND IGNORANCE OF OUR LANGUAGE AND CULTURE MADE THEM, WE THOUGHT, INFERIOR TO US. WE NEVER SAW HOW WE COULD APPEAR THAT WAY TO THEM. THAT OUR LACK OF KNOWLEDGE OF THEIR LANGUAGE AND CULTURE MADE US IGNORANT.*

BROTHERS AND SISTERS, WE NEED TO TAKE CARE OF OUR POOR, THE NATIVE WOMEN, AND THEIR CHILDREN.

WE TRIED TO DRESS THEM LIKE OURSELVES AND TEACH THEM ENGLISH.

PRES. SESSIONS- WHAT IS OUR QUOTA OF PETTICOATS AND WHITE SHIRTS WE NEED TO MAKE?

WHO DID YOU STEAL THIS FROM? **

I BOUGHT THIS SHIRT, IT'S MINE.

NO!

NO, ITS NOT! GIVE IT TO US

*The Book of Mormon is a story about the ancient inhabitants of the Americas. The members of the church typically assumed that any Native in the Americas was a descendant of this ancient people. *A House Full of Females, Plural Marriage and Women's Rights in Early Mormonism, 1835-1870,* Laurel Thatcher Ulrich, PS,p. 205.
**According to Brigham H. Roberts, in Utah Valley during the winter of 1850, a native known as Old Bishop was accused of wearing the shirt of a Mormon from Fort Utah (Provo). Ordered to remove the shirt and hand it over, Old Bishop refused to do so, protesting that he had purchased the shirt. During the ensuing skirmish, one of the whites shot the Indian, disemboweled and filled his body with stones, and threw it into the Provo River. This started a war between the Natives and the whites known as "Battle at Fort Utah." Brigham Young, convinced by Isaac Higby, Parley P. Pratt and Willard Richards, gave the Nauvoo Legion permission to kill any "hostile" Timpanogos people. They killed around 100 natives. Patty's horses were recruited for the war. (*Comprehensive History*, 3:467-76)PS page 143 footnote. (https://en.wikipedia.org/wiki/Battle_at_Fort_Utah).

THE SETTLERS'S STRUGGLE WITH THE NATIVES CONTINUED.

SISTER SESSIONS, WE ARE AT WAR WITH THE INDIANS DOWN SOUTH AND NEED YOUR HORSES FOR THE EFFORT!**

SHOULD WE GIVE THEM THEIR SHIRTS BEFORE OR AFTER YOU SHOOT THEM?

SATURDAY, AUGUST 11TH 1855.
HARRIET DELIVERED TWIN BOYS IN THE SPAN OF THREE DAYS TIME.*

THAT HAD TO HAVE BEEN THE LONGEST LABOR IN HISTORY.

I THINK YOU'RE RIGHT!

PATTY, THE SECOND TWIN, BERNARD, IS SICK, CAN YOU COME BLESS HIM?

JOHN, I DON'T FEEL WELL MYSELF... HOW ABOUT YOU GIVE ME A BLESSING FIRST?

* Harriet had a difficult labor. Patty wrote that Harriet had "a very difficult case as she had a blood vessel broke when the first was born and was badly tore and injured..." Patty then took care of Harriet's other kids and household duties as well as others calling for her to treat them. PS, p.219

HARRIET AND THE CHILDREN HAVE LITTLE BESIDE CORNBREAD TO EAT.

WELL, DON'T LET THEM SUFFER, IF YOU ALL COME AND LIVE WITH ME, YOU WILL FARE AS WELL AS I DO.

WHAT I HAVE, I HAVE PROVIDED FOR BY MYSELF.

HMMM, NEVER MIND.*

SISTER SESSIONS, CAN YOU COME TO ELIZABETH'S AID? SHE IS SOON TO DELIVER.

YES.... JUST A MINUTE, AND I'LL BE READY.

WORK RESUMED AS USUAL. THERE IS NO REST FOR THE RIGHTEOUS.

*John did ask Patty to support Harriet more, and she told him it made more sense to live in one home, not two, to combine resources. John gave her no reply and never brought Harriet to live with her. PS, p.228

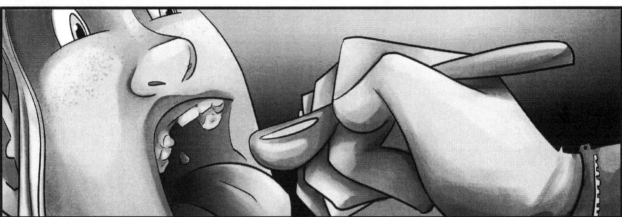

*Patty's first husband David's second plural wife was named Harriet as was her second (if you don't count Joseph) husband's plural wife.

*Patty's daughter Sylvia, much to Patty's happiness, eventually made it over the Wasatch Mountains into Utah.

AN OLD JAR OF PEACHES NEVER HURT ANYONE...

AFTER BREAKFAST ONE MORNING, I WAS TAKEN CAPTIVE BY THE DESTROYER.

TRULY, I WAS SO SICK THAT IT HAD TO HAVE BEEN LUCIFER HIMSELF COME TO GET ME.

oOOooOOHHOHHH OOHHHHHHHHH

RUMBLE RUMBLE

JOHN!! THE DEVIL HIMSELF HAS TAKEN ME!!

IT FEELS LIKE I SWALLOWED A BEAR TRAP! WILL YOU GIVE ME A BLESSING?

OOOAA AOAOAO AOAOHH

WELL, THAT DIDN'T WORK.

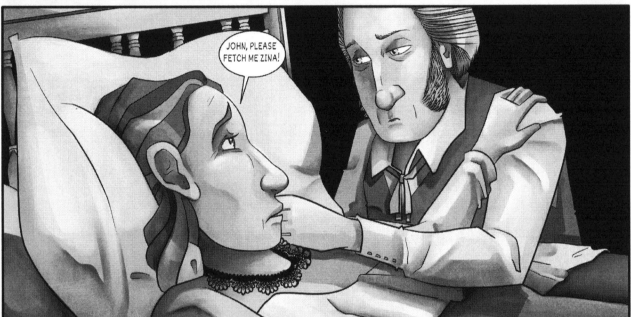

*Patty really thought the destroyer had overtaken her, but in reading her journal, it seems she may have eaten bad peaches from an improperly sealed jar. PS, p.302

*Sylvia's 4th husband husband Ezekiel Clark was the first originator of this idea who recommended it to President Lincoln's treasury. PS, p.310
**ZCMI-Zion's Cooperative Mercantile Institution was the first department store in the United States. It was founded on October 9, 1868 by Brigham Young. For many years it used the slogan, "America's First Department Store"

1868

*Olive H. Walker, Adah Phipin, and Sophia Tripp asked Patty to take charge of a straw braiding school, and to also "take care" of the braid and the straw.
**Meeting notes found on page 406 of her diary.

January 1868: John Parry died.
He had been sick over a year. Suffered more than tongue can tell.
In all his sickness he was patient, more so than any person I ever saw. I never heard a murmur from his lips. Died without a struggle or a groan. A good man, a kind husband, a tender father and a good Latter Day Saint.*

*Patty did not have so many nice things to say about her first husband David any time after his death. She did sell a home and lot in exchange for his gravestone though.

PARRY
JOHN
1789–1868
BORN IN NORTH WALES

PERRIGRINE AND I TOOK A TRIP BACK TO MAINE TO VISIT ALL MY RELATIVES THAT I HAD NOT SEEN FOR 34 YEARS. WE TRAVELED NEARLY 7,000 MILES BY RAILROAD, STAGE, AND CARRIAGES. IT COST ME $500, AND I DON'T REGRET A SINGLE PENNY.

I CAN'T BELIEVE WHAT TOOK US MONTHS WILL ONLY TAKE A FEW DAYS NOW!

THIS SURE IS A NICE CHANGE.

ENOCH! IT WARMS MY HEART TO SEE YOU.

OH PATTY! YOU'RE STILL ALIVE!

YOU KNOW, YOU WOULD HAVE LIVED AN EASIER LIFE IF YOU WOULD HAVE JUST STAYED HERE.

NO, NO, ENOCH. ALL THE PAIN AND SUFFERING WERE WORTH IT.

I HAD JUST MISSED SEEING MY MOTHER BY TWO YEARS.

I SUPPOSE IF I AM ABLE TO LIVE AS LONG AS YOU DID MOTHER, I HAVE 25 MORE YEARS LEFT.

THAT'S A WHOLE OTHER LIFE!

*In trying to compile all the stories throughout this novel and more so in the last years of her life, rearrangements of when some things happened have been made. For cold hard dates, you'd need to refer to her actual diary.
**Patty did take joy rides in her new buggy, but never displayed or bragged about her wealth.
***This would be like building a home for $68,700 in today's money, and paying cash for it. Patty moved to Bountiful, the city her son Perrigrine established, to be closer to family.
****In today's dollars $16,000 would be worth $326,613.

I WAS PROUD OF HOW MUCH I WAS ABLE TO CONTRIBUTE TO THE "BUILDING UP OF ZION!"*

LOGAN TEMPLE **

I WAS SOMEWHAT OF THE TOWN BANKER. SOME PAID ME BACK WITH INTEREST, SOME JUST PAID ME BACK, AND SOME NOT AT ALL. OTHERS I GAVE TO AS GIFTS AND DIDN'T EXPECT MONEY IN RETURN.***

*This Salt Lake Temple donation would be $86,460 in today's money. "Zion" was a word used to describe the end goal of what the members wanted to achieve. It meant, "one heart and one mind" for the people. In reading Patty's journal and her interaction with others and her observations of others, shows that "zion" was hard to achieve and its members still struggle with its achievement today.
**Patty was the largest contributor to the construction of the Logan Temple of those who did not live in or near Logan City. (Logan Temple: The First 100 Years, Nolan Porter Olsen.) *She was given a letter by then President John Taylor and counselor George Q. Cannon, inviting her to the building's dedication. This was a great honor for Patty.
***Patty helped her son Perrigrine's wives complete the costs of building their own separate homes. As often as possible, women in plural marriages sought out having their own homes. The husband then took turns living with them.

DON'T WORRY SALLY, I'LL SEE TO IT THAT YOU HAVE A HOME TO RAISE YOUR FAMILY IN.

OH CARLOS* GRUMBLE, GRUMBLE.

PERRIGRINE WAS PROLIFIC. OR RATHER HIS NINE WIVES WERE. HE EVENTUALLY HAD A TOTAL OF 55 CHILDREN, ALL OF WHOM NEEDED A GOOD EDUCATION. **

I DECIDED TO PAY FOR THE BUILDING OF THE PATTY SESSIONS ACADEMY AND HELPED EMPLOY THOSE THAT TAUGHT THERE.***

FUTURE HOME OF THE

PATTY SESSIONS ACADEMY

PATTY SESSIONS ACADEMY

HURRAY FOR GRANDMA PATTY!

1885

MY LIFE STARTED TO WIND DOWN. I GAVE ADVICE TO OTHER WOMEN ON MIDWIFERY, BUT SPENT MOST OF MY DAYS AT MY LOOM OR KNITTING.

**Carlos was Patty's grandson and Sally was Carlos' third of four wives. Patty indeed built Sally's home because Carlos was not taking care of her and their kids. The need for Patty to provide for the plural wives of her first and second husband, her son, and her grandson demonstrates that polygamy was not completely about improving the socioeconomic status of the widow and fatherless. In fact, plural marriage more often than not led to women receiving less support from their spouse. However, women and men were taught that a plural marriage was more noble spiritually and led to a "higher" reward in heaven, thus some women turned down an opportunity to have their very own husband in return for being a lonely plural wife. *A Mormon Mother; An autobiography.* Annie Clark Tanner.
**Jean Stringham Green, Patty's great-great- granddaughter grew up in Bountiful Utah and commented that it was nice to find a boy to date that she wasn't related to. Accounts of Patty paying a school teacher can be found in her journal. PS, p 343-349.

*** The schoolhouse dedication was held on 15 December, the meeting was called to order by Brother Henry Rampton, and the dedicatory prayer was offered by P.G. Sessions. As she addressed the meeting, Patty named a board of directors: P.G. Sessions; John Fisher, who was married to her granddaughter Josephine; and [Joseph Lamoni] Holbrook. Patty explained that she had $16,000 invested in ZCMI at Salt Lake City. The school committee were to see that a sufficient portion of the dividends was kept out to pay the expenses of the school. The building was described as "a brick building 18x36, with twelve-foot ceiling and well finished and furnished." An Article, "Patty Sessions' School" in the *Deseret Evening News* of 20 December 1883. PS, p. 396

I WOVE THE OLD SHAWL PIECES INTO A RUG.

DEAR LORD....I AM REMINDED EVERY DAY HOW YOU HAVE BROUGHT US OUT OF TRIAL AND GIVEN US A GOOD LIFE.

I WAS ADMITTEDLY VERY HARD OF HEARING TOWARDS THE END OF MY LIFE.

I OFTEN MADE SOCKS TO PASS THE TIME, BUT MY OLD FINGERS AND EYESIGHT CAUSED MANY DROPPED STITCHES.

HERE IS SOME MORE YARN FOR YOU!

WHAAAAAT??

THEY SURE DO NEED A LOT OF SOCKS.

FAMILY WOULD UNRAVEL THE SOCKS AND RETURN THE YARN FOR ME TO KEEP KNITTING.

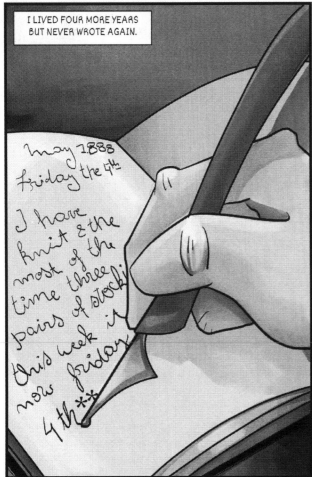

I LIVED FOUR MORE YEARS BUT NEVER WROTE AGAIN.

May 1888
Friday the 4th

I have knit & the most of the time three pairs of stocki this week is now friday 4th**

Deseret Evening News, December 14th, 1892

OBITUARIES

"Almost 100"
Patty Bartlett Sessions

Died at her home at 6:30 o'clock this Wednesday morning of old age.

*Betsy, Elizabeth Birdenow, was Perrigrine's sixth wife. She had one stillborn birth of a daughter and no other children of her own. She lived with and took care of Patty until Patty passed. Patty speaks of Betsy often in her journals with affection.
**Patty actually wrote this as her last journal entry. She died four years later at the age of 97.
***At the time of Patty's death, she had a total posterity of 214. To count the total number today, would take more effort than this author, Patty's 4th great granddaughter, cares to give.

THE END.

SOURCES

Books

Smart, Donna Toland. *Mormon Midwife The 1846-1888 Diaries of Patty Bartlett Sessions*, Logan, Utah, Utah State University Press. 1997

Ulrich, Laurel Thatcher. *A House Full of Females: Plural Marriage and Women's Rights in Early Mormonism,1835-1870*, New York, Vintage Books. 2017

Smart, Donna Toland. *Exemplary Elder The Life and Missionary Diaries of Perrigrine Sessions 1814-1893*, Provo, Utah BYU Studies and the Joseph Fielding Smith Institute for Latter-day Saint History. 2002

Thomas, William. *Animal Simples, Approved for Modern Uses and Cures*. London. Bristol: John Wright & Co. 1899. pg 457

Joseph Smith History, 1838-1856, vol.D-1. https://www.josephsmithpapers.org/paper-summary/history-1838-1856-volume-d-1-1-august-1842-1-july-1843/185

Ferris, Mrs. B.G. *Mormons at Home*. New York. DIX & Edwards. 1856

Olsen, Nolan Porter. *Logan Temple: The First 100 Years*. Providence, Utah: K.W. Watkins, 1979, ©1978

Tanner, Annie Clark. *A Mormon Mother, An Autobiography: Annie Clark Tanner*. Salt Lake City, Utah. Signature Books. 1983

Magazines and Newspapers

Women's Exponent issues: 13 (September 1,1884) 51:13 (September 15, 1884): 63;13 (November 1, 1884):86;13 (November 15, 1884): 94-95;13 (February 1, 1885): 134-35; 13 (March 1, 1885): 150-51;14 (June 1, 1885):2,14 (November 15, 1885):85-86,94-95.)

Nielson,Quig. "Patty Sessions Delivered 3,977 Babies as a Midwife," *Davis County Clipper*, 2 March 1992, quoting Kate B. Carter, ed. Our Pioneer Heritage (Salt Lake City: Daughters of Utah Pioneers, 1959), 2:426

Patty Sessions' School, Deseret Evening News. 20 December 1883.

Websites

www.ourworlddata.org

https://www.nationalgeographic.com/culture/food/the-plate/2014/04/21/
how-was-ketchup-invented/

https://education.jlab.org › itselemental › ele030

https://www.thornber.net/medicine/html/medgloss.html
https://en.wikipedia.org/wiki/Battle_at_Fort_Utah

https://en.wikipedia.org/wiki/Missouri_Executive_Order_44

https://en.wikipedia.org/wiki/Winter_Quarters_(North_Omaha,_Nebraska

https://en.wikipedia.org/wiki/Mormon_Battalion

https://en.wikipedia.org/wiki/Utah_War

Made in United States
Troutdale, OR
02/13/2024